THE BEST
GRAND
JUNCTION
HIKES

THE WESTERN SLOPE GROUP
of
THE COLORADO MOUNTAIN CLUB
with
ROD MARTINEZ

The Colorado Mountain Club Press
Golden, Colorado

The Best Grand Junction Hikes
© 2012 by The Colorado Mountain Club

PUBLISHED BY

The Colorado Mountain Club Press
710 Tenth Street, Suite 200, Golden, Colorado 80401
303-996-2743   e-mail: cmcpress@cmc.org

Founded in 1912, The Colorado Mountain Club is the largest outdoor recreation, education, and conservation organization in the Rocky Mountains. Look for our books at your local bookstore or outdoor retailer or online at www.cmc.org/books.

     Alan Bernhard: design, composition, and production
     John Gascoyne: series editor
     Rod Martinez: project manager
     Alan Stark: publisher

CONTACTING THE PUBLISHER
We would appreciate it if readers would alert us to any errors or outdated information by contacting us at the address above.

DISTRIBUTED TO THE BOOK TRADE BY
The Mountaineers Books, 1001 SW Klickitat Way, Suite 201, Seattle, WA 98134, 800-553-4453, www.mountaineersbooks.org

TOPOGRAPHIC MAPS are copyright 2009 and were created using National Geographic TOPO! Outdoor Recreation software (www.natgeomaps.com; 800-962-1643).

COVER PHOTO: Independence Monument is a freestanding tower of soft, red sandstone, which soars 450 feet above the floor of Monument Canyon in the Colorado National Monument. This view, with Grand Junction in the background, is from Rim Rock Drive in the Colorado National Monument. Photo by Rod Martinez.

We gratefully acknowledge the financial support of the people of Colorado through the Scientific and Cultural Facilities District of greater metropolitan Denver for our publishing activities.

WARNING: Although there has been an effort to make the trail descriptions in this book as accurate as possible, some discrepancies may exist between the text and the trails in the field. Hiking in mountainous areas, and canyons and deserts as well, is a high-risk activity. This guidebook is not a substitute for your experience and common sense. The users of this guidebook assume full responsibility for their own safety. Weather, terrain conditions, and individual abilities must be considered before undertaking any of the hikes in this guide.

First Edition

ISBN 978-1-937052-00-3

Printed in China

THIS BOOK IS DEDICATED TO SOME GREAT HIKING FRIENDS, Mike Partyka, Jerry Shallman, and Mike Smith, as well as to my wife, Sue—who now has in writing where I have been part of the last 40-plus years. This book also highlights many of the trails my sons, John and Chris, have accompanied me on. Most importantly, it is dedicated to my granddaughters Brittany, Nichole, and Samantha, and other young people. I hope they will enjoy the outdoors and photographing it to share in the beauty that surrounds us as much as I have.

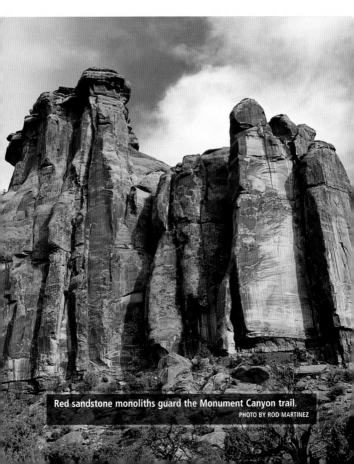

Red sandstone monoliths guard the Monument Canyon trail.
PHOTO BY ROD MARTINEZ

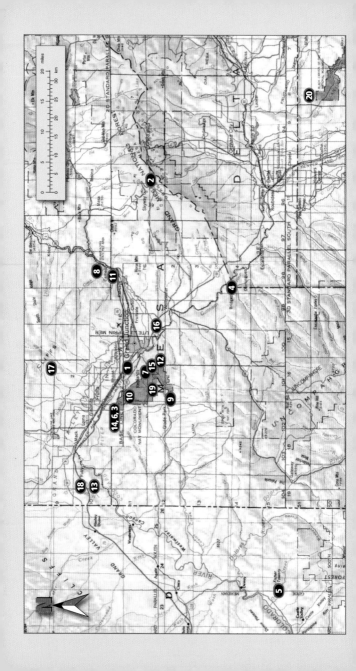

CONTENTS

ACKNOWLEDGMENTS

For you to be able to enjoy this pack guide, it took the efforts of the following people to hike and write the trail narratives, take the photos, and chart the maps:

Larry Allison	Carol Butler
Dave Butler	Lon Carpenter
Allan Conrad	Carolyn Emanuel
Joyce Frost	John Gascoyne
Dave Hanley	Mike Madachy
Mary McCutchan	Babs Schmerler

Without these folks persevering and volunteering their valuable time, this pack guide would not have been accomplished. Other Western Slope Group members who came to the aid of the pack guide are Rick Emanuel for the use of his photos and Larry Allison for mapping the Tellerico Trail.

Without the support and encouragement of all the Western Slope Group members, this pack guide would have been a task and not a pleasure. Thanks to Alan Stark, publisher at The Colorado Mountain Press, for his expert guidance and terrific selection of the cover photo. The biggest thanks must go to John Gascoyne, series editor. His help to a novice author and reworking of written efforts took away the challenge and self-imposed frustration. Along with the many back-and-forth exchanges of material, we also shared our personal hiking efforts and resulting aches and pains. Thanks again, John.

Happy trails to all!

Foreword

The Western Slope Group of The Colorado Mountain Club welcomes you to Grand Junction and the Western Slope of Colorado. The 20 hikes in this pack guide, selected by Western Slope members, are unique because you have the ability to do all but one of them year round.

A large portion of the Western Slope is high desert, and snow is limited to the high country of the Grand Mesa. The Grand Mesa is also a great place to crosscountry ski or snowshoe. This pack guide will let you experience a national park—Black Canyon—and the Colorado National Monument. These two areas are set aside to preserve the unique beauty found on the Western Slope.

On your way to the top of the Grand Mesa, you will hike an area that has an abundance of flora and fauna not often found in other areas of the state. The hike to the top of Mount Garfield will give you outstanding views to the east, including the Elk Mountains; the San Juans directly to the south; and the Bookcliff Mountains that stretch for over 200 miles from Mount Garfield into eastern Utah.

It seems as if the sun is always shining in Grand Junction, which should lead to caution about almost all the hikes in this guide. It is always best to start hiking early in the morning and try to finish by early afternoon in order to avoid the peak heat of the day and the afternoon thunderstorms as well.

Most of the hikes are in the high desert, so extra water is recommended to counter both the heat and the dryness. Bug spray is also recommended in the spring and summer to avoid all those insects that wish to bite or sting you. Sunscreen is also a good idea for most of the high desert and canyon country hikes.

This pack guide details only 20 hikes in the Grand Junction area, but there are a myriad of other hikes and outdoor activities that you can enjoy. After your hike, take time to visit a fruit orchard or winery to participate in the other "fruits" of the Grand Valley.

ROD MARTINEZ,
author, photographer, group member, treasurer
Western Slope Group, The Colorado Mountain Club

Enjoy a walk down the old Grand Mesa road. PHOTO BY ROD MARTINEZ

INTRODUCTION

The city of Grand Junction was founded where two great rivers, the Gunnison and the Colorado, join together to continue the journey of the Colorado to the Gulf of California. *The Best Grand Junction Hikes* pack guide will take you from the heights of the Grand Mesa and Mount Garfield to the depths of the Black Canyon, as well as along the banks of the Colorado River.

The junction of the two rivers is also the heart of the Grand Valley and the heart of this pack guide as well. As you read this guide you will note exciting diversity in the types of trails and terrain available. While most of these hikes can be hiked any time of the year, you'll learn seasons and reasons that will optimize your choices.

The Grand Mesa, which is the world's largest flat-top mesa, dominates the east end of the Valley. It's over 10,000 feet above sea level and more than 40 miles long. Visit Grand Mesa in the fall for spectacular golden aspen leaves or in the winter to enjoy cross-country skiing or snowshoeing in the deep snow.

To really experience the Grand Mesa, hike one of many trails, with your ultimate objective being the Crag Crest trail. From the top of this trail your views are almost limitless—to the San Juan Mountains to the south and to the east the Bookcliffs reaching almost 200 miles into northwest Utah.

Mount Garfield dominates the skyline in the northwest corner of the Grand Valley. The 2,000-foot hike to the top culminates in another spectacular view of the Grand Valley, the Colorado National Monument and, farther west, to the La Sal Mountains and eastern Utah.

The Black Canyon of the Gunnison National Park is to the south of Grand Junction, near Montrose. At Warner Point on the South Rim Drive of the canyon, the Gunnison River is 2,772 feet below the cliff rim. A great way to experience the full depth of the canyon is to hike the Ute Trail, as described in this guide. The trail descends gradually to the river, where you will have impressive views of the towering cliffs and the Gunnison Gorge's double canyon.

Most of the hikes in this pack guide focus on the unique and beautiful red rock country of Western Colorado. Dominguez Canyon offers waterfalls and petroglyphs. History is relived along the Gunnison Bluffs and Spanish Trail. The guide's most western trail is in eastern Utah at the base of the majestic La Sal Mountains. The Fisher Towers trail will take you to the base of the "Titan," a 900-foot-tall tower that is made of crumbly, difficult-to-climb rock. The 360-degree panoramic view at the end of the trail is well worth the 4.4-mile round-trip hike.

Back in Colorado, a number of hikes start in the Colorado National Monument as well as the McInnis Canyons National Conservation Area. The Pollock Bench and Rattlesnake Canyon trails will take you to the base of the largest concentration of arches outside of Arches National Park. In this area there are 11 arches, with 9 of them concentrated in a 1.0-mile stretch of the canyon. The landscape of the Colorado National Monument is a fascinating mix of plateaus, canyons, cliffs, and towering monoliths up to 500 feet tall. The Monument Canyon trail descends 600 feet down into the main canyon of the Colorado National Monument, where you will hike by the Kissing Couple, the Coke Ovens, and the iconic Independence Rock.

Wildlife is both abundant and diverse in the Grand Valley. Perhaps most exciting are the wild horses you may encounter on the Tellerico or Main Canyon trails, or on top of Mount Garfield. The Grand Mesa provides habitat for black bear, elk, deer, and the ever-elusive moose. As you hike in the red rock country of Western Colorado, you may meet up with rattlesnakes, scorpions, bobcats, coyotes, mountain lions, or Desert Bighorn Sheep.

The Desert Bighorn Sheep, a frequent early morning riser. PHOTO BY ROD MARTINEZ

John Otto, first superintendent of Colorado National Monument, was a fierce and persistent advocate of having the red rock country turned into a national park. Today he would be proud to hike the Monument and the other trails of the Grand Valley and surrounding areas.

As you use and enjoy this pack guide in 2012, celebrate with us the 100th anniversary of The Colorado Mountain Club—the largest and oldest hiking and climbing organization in the Rocky Mountains. We are also all about conservation of our precious natural resources. New members with any level of hiking ability—from novice to expert—are most welcome to join us. Information is available at www.cmc.org.

An extraordinary Fisher Tower.   PHOTO BY ROD MARTINEZ

THE TEN ESSENTIALS SYSTEM

The Colorado Mountain Club, through the Colorado Mountain Club Press, is the publisher of this pack guide. For 100 years The Colorado Mountain Club has fostered safety awareness and safe practices in the wilderness. In order to benefit from these concepts, all hikers are encouraged to study, adopt, and teach The Ten Essentials System as part of their own outdoors regimen.

1. **Hydration.** Carry at least two liters or quarts of water on any hike. For arid country or desert hiking, carry more. Keep an extra water container in your vehicle and hydrate both before and after your hike. Don't wait until you are thirsty—stay hydrated.

2. **Nutrition.** Eat a good breakfast before your hike; pack a full and healthy lunch, including fruits, vegetables, and carbohydrates. Carry such healthy snacks as trail mix and nutrition bars.

3. **Sun protection.** Start with sunscreen with an SPF rating of at least 45 and reapply it as you hike. Wear sunglasses, a wide-brimmed hat, and use lip balm. These protections are important anywhere in Colorado, especially so in our desert areas.

4. **Insulation (extra clothing).** Be aware that weather in Colorado can go through extreme changes in very short amounts of time. Think warm; think dry—even in arid areas. Dress with wool or synthetic inner and outer layers. Cotton retains moisture and does not insulate well; it should not be part of your hiking gear. Carry a warm hat, gloves, and extra socks. Always include a rain/wind parka and rain pants—on you or in your pack. Extra clothing weighs little and is a great safety component.

5. **Navigation.** You want to attain at least minimal proficiency with a map and compass. A GPS unit can add to your ability, but it's not a substitute for the two basics. Before a hike, study your route, and the surrounding country, on a good map of the area.

6. **Illumination.** Include a headlamp or flashlight in your gear, preferably both. With a headlamp, your hands are kept free. Avoid hiking in the darkness if at all possible.

7. **First-aid supplies.** Buy or assemble an adequate first-aid kit. Some things to include: Ace bandages; a bandana—which can double as a sling; duct tape—good as a bandage, blister protection, or for rips in your clothes; a small bottle of alcohol or hydrogen peroxide for cleaning a wound; latex gloves; specific medications for you or your companions; toilet paper and Ziploc bags for carrying it out. Note: this is not a comprehensive list—tailor it and add items for your own perceived needs and intended activities.

8. **Fire.** The best practice is to avoid open fires except in emergency situations. For when you may need to build a fire: carry waterproof matches in a watertight container, a lighter, or a commercial fire starter such as a fire ribbon. Keep these items dry and ensure that all of them will work in cold or wet weather. If needed, tree sap or dry pine needles can help start a fire.

9. **Repair kit and emergency tools.** A pocketknife or multi-tool and duct tape or electrician's tape are all good for various repairs. For emergencies, carry a whistle and signal mirror.

10. **Emergency shelter.** Carry a space blanket and nylon cord or a bivouac sack. Large plastic leaf bags are handy for temporary rain gear, pack covers, or survival shelters. On your way out, use this for trash left by more careless hikers.

Looking down Ute Canyon.

Some additional safety measures:

- **Tell someone** where you plan to go on your hike and when you plan to return.

- **Leave a note** on your dashboard, readable from outside your vehicle and providing information about your hike—where you plan to go, when you will return, how many people are in your party, contact information for family or friends, etc.

- **Bring a Spot** along on your hike. In an emergency, this personal locator device can tell emergency personnel where you are and that you need their help. When not hiking, keep this beacon device in your vehicle—just in case.

1. Connected Lakes Trail

BY ROD MARTINEZ

MAPS	Trails Illustrated, Grand Junction/Fruita, Number 502 USGS, Grand Junction, 7.5 minute
ELEVATION GAIN	Minimal
RATING	Easy
ROUND-TRIP DISTANCE	1.5 miles
ROUND-TRIP TIME	1 hour
NEAREST LANDMARK	Highway 340, Grand Junction

COMMENT: The James M. Robb–Colorado River State Park encompasses a number of trails from Island Acres on the eastern edge of the Colorado River corridor to the Fruita section and Loma boat launch on the western edge of the corridor.

The Connected Lakes section offers great pathways for walking or hiking, fishing, picnicking, and bird watching. This section runs along the banks of the Colorado River, where you can hike close to and around Duke Lake, Endangered Fish Lake, and both sections of Connected Lakes.

As you hike or walk the paved and hard-pack trails, look for wildlife, which can include skunks, beaver, or a rarely seen but nonetheless in-the-neighborhood mountain lion. Bring your binoculars to get a close look at the great variety of birds that can be found in the park. On a recent hike, I spotted four large turkey buzzards roosting in a large dead cottonwood tree. Stop, listen, and enjoy the varied songs of many species of birds as they communicate with one another.

Take some time to visit the Grand Valley Audubon Trail, the Luci Ferril Ela Wildlife Sanctuary, or make your way across the Colorado River (via another route not described here) to walk the 1.5 mile Blue Heron Trail.

GETTING THERE: From the intersection of 1st Street, Grand Avenue, and Hwy 50 (on the northwest side of the downtown section of Grand Junction), travel west on Hwy 340 for about 1.0 mile,

One of many lakes at the Connected Lakes section of the
James M. Robb–Colorado River State Park.

PHOTO BY ROD MARTINEZ

where the road will intersect with Dike Road. Turn right onto
Dike Road and follow it for 1.5 miles to the entrance of the
Connected Lakes section of the James M. Robb–Colorado River
State Park. An entrance fee of $6.00 or Colorado State Parks pass
is required for all vehicles. From the entrance, travel 0.3 mile to
the Kingfisher parking lot. Restroom facilities are available.

THE ROUTE: This is the easiest trail in this pack guide. The trail is
concrete, paved, or hard-packed dirt and gravel and is accessible
by wheelchairs.

From the restroom area, follow the concrete path to a larger
concrete path. Go right at this junction and follow the concrete
path for almost 0.5 mile to Promontory Point. Then retrace your
steps for about 100 yards and take a left onto the hard-packed
dirt and gravel trail. In about 200 yards you will intersect with a
trail that takes you, via "The Causeway," between Connected
Lakes and Endangered Fish Lake. Stay left on the dirt trail and
continue on the Waterfowl Loop trail.

In about another 0.25 mile, another trail on the right will take
you to Osprey Point. After doing this short loop, return to the

A turkey buzzard is one of many birds viewable in the park.

PHOTO BY ROD MARTINEZ

Waterfowl Loop trail for the last 0.25 mile walk back to your vehicle.

There are a number of benches and short side trails to the lakes and the Colorado River. Take the time to enjoy the whole park as well as the serenity that an early morning hike at Connected Lakes will provide for you.

Endangered Fish Lake.

PHOTO BY ROD MARTINEZ

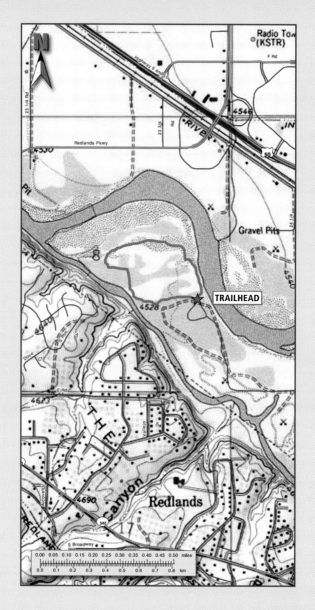

2. Crag Crest

BY MIKE MADACHY

MAPS	Trails Illustrated, Grand Mesa, Number 136 USGS, Grand Mesa, 7.5 minute
ELEVATION GAIN	1,000 feet
RATING	Moderate
ROUND-TRIP DISTANCE	10.4 miles
ROUND-TRIP TIME	4.5–6 hours
NEAREST LANDMARK	Grand Mesa

COMMENT: The Grand Mesa is a large, flat-topped mountain that is home to hundreds of lakes found between 10,000 and 11,000 feet in elevation. During winter months, the Grand Mesa is a snowy paradise with world-class crosscountry skiing. The snow accumulation, significant in the winter, can last until June. Hiking the Crag Crest trail is primarily a summer and fall activity. At 11,189 feet, it is the highest trek in this guide and makes for a cool escape on a hot summer day.

From the crest, over a dozen lakes can be seen on a clear day, along with views of the Elk Mountains, the San Juan Mountains, the La Sal Mountains in Utah, and the Bookcliffs. The lower portion of the trail is comprised of forest and open meadows. A myriad of wildflowers brightens the meadows in summer.

The most popular starting point is the west trailhead. It is recommended that you ascend the crest first and then return on the lower loop. Be aware that afternoon thunderstorms can appear quickly. The crest is exposed to weather and is a poor place to be during a lightning storm, so plan to get an early start.

From the west, a trailhead to Cottonwood Lake trail and the lower loops is open to bikes and horses. The upper crest is reserved for hikers. During summer months, bugs can appear in significant numbers. Bring both bug protection and sunscreen.

GETTING THERE: About 20 minutes east of Grand Junction on I-70, take exit 49 and go south on Hwy 65 (Grand Mesa National Scenic and Historic Byway) for about 32 miles. This beautiful

Wildflowers bloom throughout the summer.

PHOTO BY MIKE MADACHY

drive winds through the town of Mesa and ascends to over 10,000 feet. Just a few hundred feet past mile marker 28, the West Craig trailhead parking is on the left (north) side of the road. The trailhead has restrooms and ample free parking.

THE ROUTE: From the east end of the parking lot, the trail ascends northeast along colorful meadows of wildflowers. At 0.4 mile the trail splits to the left for the crest and to the right for the lower loop. If the weather looks clear, turn left and do the crest first, for a clockwise loop. All of the following trail descriptions are based on your making this clockwise loop. If the sky looks ominous, you could still do the lower loop before bad weather sets in.

Enjoy views of the meadows while ascending. At 2.7 miles from the trailhead, the first glimpse of the other side is visible. The ridge is steep on both sides. The next several miles offer spectacular views from the crest. Terrain can alternate from rough rock trails and grassy areas to pockets of trees. Lakes visible to the south include the Hotel lakes, Butts Lake, Eggleston

Lake, and Baron Lake. The West Elk range and San Juan Mountains are visible to the east and south. Looking to the west you can see the Uncompahgre Plateau and La Sal Mountains in Utah.

The highest point of your hike—11,184 feet—is reached at 3.9 miles. The trail starts its southern descent after 4.6 miles and winds past Bullfinch Reservoir, on the left, then along Upper Eggleston Lake. The trail next takes a southwestern heading and the terrain changes to forest. Portions of the lower loop have suffered from windstorms that have resulted in many downed trees. The downed wood is habitat for spruce beetles, which are on the increase. Starting at mile 7, the fallen trees are abundant. At about 8.4 miles, when the trail turns left, a short path to Forest Lake—Upper Hotel Lake on some maps—can be seen up and to the right. Be alert—this path is easy to miss. As you continue west through shaded forest, several lakes are visible and picnic spots with nice views are plentiful. To complete the hike, go left at mile 10 and descend in a southwest direction back to the west trailhead parking area.

The crest, or top, is loose and steep on both sides.   PHOTO BY MIKE MADACHY

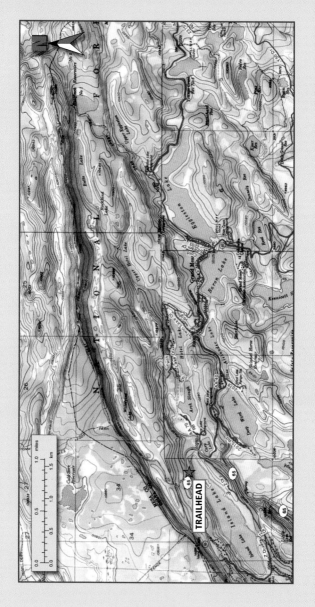

TRAILHEAD

3. Devils Canyon Trail

BY LON CARPENTER

MAPS	Trails Illustrated, Grand Junction/Fruita, Number 502
ELEVATION GAIN	650 feet
RATING	Moderate
ROUND-TRIP DISTANCE	7.0 miles
ROUND-TRIP TIME	4–5 hours
NEAREST LANDMARK	Town of Fruita

COMMENT: Devils Canyon is an outstanding day hike, through a deep red rock canyon of Wingate sandstone. The trail loops around a second canyon, cut into the darker bedrock, which is much older than the surrounding canyon walls. The trail winds around through juniper and piñon pine trees and around weathered boulders from the same bedrock formation.

Keep an eye out for Desert Bighorn Sheep that frequently can be found in the canyon. The end of the loop circles around a small rustic cowboy cabin, used at an earlier time when cattle still grazed in the canyon. While the scenic canyon runs farther west, there is no formal trail beyond this point. As the cabin also marks the halfway point in the hike, it is a great place to take a lunch break. You may want to stop in and sign the guest register inside the cabin.

On the return leg, the view east into the Grand Valley and the Bookcliffs in the distance, framed by the deep red canyon walls, provides a striking contrast to the difference in geology between both sides of the Grand Valley.

The trail can be hiked year round. Extra water should be carried in the summer months, as the daytime temperature can reach 100 degrees. It's a good idea to keep another water container in your vehicle—to hydrate with both before and after your hike. Horses are allowed on the trails.

GETTING THERE: From Grand Junction, travel I-70 west 9 miles to Fruita exit 19. Turn left, south, onto Hwy 340 for about 1.5 miles,

Looking up the canyon.

and then turn right, into Kingsview Estates subdivision. Travel north through the subdivision 0.5 mile, or so, and turn into the signed Devils Canyon parking lot on the left.

THE ROUTE: There are many trails that start from this trailhead; watch for signposts at trail intersections. Take trail D1, an easy hike through the low hills on the approach to the canyon. At the intersection with trail D4, take D4 to the intersection with trail D3, which is in the bottom of the canyon. This point is the beginning of the loop trail section that travels into the main section of Devils Canyon. The trail steepens some past this point as it gains elevation. The trail will go up and down in the canyon.

Take the time to stop and view the canyon and canyon walls from different perspectives. At this intersection you are also entering the Black Ridge Canyon Wilderness Area. To complete the loop, retrace your steps to the D4-D3 intersection, follow D4 back to D1 to return to the trailhead.

A leaning tower alongside the trail.   PHOTO BY LON CARPENTER

Besides encountering Desert Bighorn Sheep, you may also run into wild horses and donkeys. An early start in the morning will increase your chances of viewing wildlife.

A rock pinnacle guides you back to the trailhead.   PHOTO BY LON CARPENTER

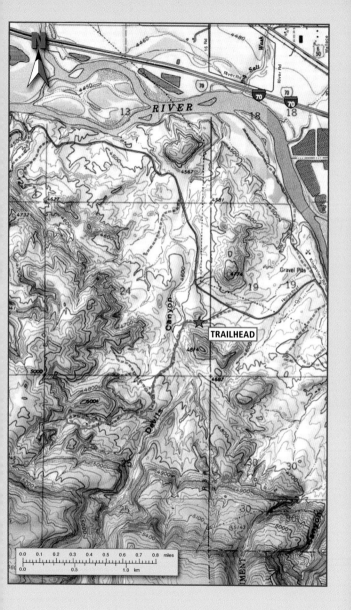

4. Dominguez Canyon Trail

BY CAROLYN EMANUEL

MAPS	USGS, Triangle Mesa, 7.5 minute
ELEVATION GAIN	Minimal
RATING	Easy
ROUND-TRIP DISTANCE	9 miles
ROUND-TRIP TIME	4–5 hours
NEAREST LANDMARK	Highway 50 south

COMMENT: Big Dominguez and Little Dominguez canyons have been carved through the sandstone of the Uncompahgre Plateau over the last 65 million years. The canyons and mesas, created by erosion, inspired the Bureau of Land Management (BLM) to preserve this area as the Dominguez Canyon Wilderness. It is the largest BLM roadless area in Colorado; its 66,280 acres contain the Dominguez-Escalante National Conservation Area.

For thousands of years Native Americans used these canyons for shelter, hunting, and as a travel corridor to the high country of the Uncompahgre Plateau. You will see evidence of these cultures on the canyon trail. The rock art sites, located on the main trail, tell the story of those who came to Dominguez Canyon before us.

The petroglyphs are Barrier Canyon rock art, dating back two millennia, with some later images of Ute Indians on horseback as well. You'll see depicted hunting weapons known as atlatls, Desert Bighorn Sheep, deer, coyotes, migration symbols, and running rivers on the large boulders. Please don't touch the rock patina as human contact can degrade the rock art. The more recent images of Utes on horseback may date to the 1880s. Early miners and settlers followed, leaving their mark in the canyon as well.

GETTING THERE: From Grand Junction, travel south on Hwy 50 for approximately 17 miles to the Bridgeport Road turnoff (CO Rd.39.50) and turn right. Drive 4.5 miles on a rough dirt road to the parking area by the railroad tracks. The footbridge is 1.0

Petroglyphs are the highlight in Dominguez Canyon.   PHOTO BY RICK EMANUEL

mile upriver from the parking area. There is a toilet facility at the parking area.

THE ROUTE: This trail begins at the Bridgeport footbridge over the Gunnison River, but it is a 1.0 mile hike upriver along the railroad tracks from your car to the footbridge. The trail is wide and easy to follow as it winds along the banks of the Gunnison River for about 0.5 mile. Note the new cottonwoods—planted by Colorado Mountain Club members.

As you cross the footbridge, remember that only horses and hikers are allowed on the trail—no mountain bikes. Once across the bridge, you'll follow the Big Dominguez Canyon trail west, past outstanding red sandstone canyons and mudstone cliffs, then jagged black bedrock of gneiss, schist, and granite. The bedrock is Precambrian, some 1.5 billion years old, whereas the sedimentary layers of the canyon walls are only one-tenth as old. Look for the most outstanding petroglyphs, 0.9 mile upstream from the confluence of Little Dominguez and Big Dominguez creeks.

On the canyon walls, you'll also see cliffs with another panel of petroglyphs. This area could be thought of as a

A bridge over the Gunnison River lends access
to Dominguez Canyon.

communications center for those who came before, and their
messages are told in the petroglyphs on these rocks.

The 2,000-year-old petroglyphs, some historic cowboy corrals
and dugouts, and a beautiful set of waterfalls are about a mile up
from the confluence of Big and Little Dominguez Creeks. Farther
on, the trail wanders past magnificent alcoves filled with box-
car-sized boulders and, on occasion, Desert Bighorn Sheep.
These sheep were hunted to extinction in this area of Colorado
in the late 19th century. In the 1980s the BLM reintroduced this
majestic native species to its original home in the canyons. The
sheep will tolerate our presence; however, hiking off trails
around the sheep increases their stress levels and hiking off
trails with a dog near the sheep is discouraged. There are many
other wildlife species in this area, including rattlesnakes, which
you will want to avoid.

Wander to the intersection of the Cactus Park trailhead at
about mile 4.5. Look for the 1907 Archie Smith (his name is
inscribed on a nearby boulder) gold mine about 50 feet below
the trail near the mining equipment. When you've considered
how rugged Mr. Smith must have been, leisurely hike back to the
Gunnison River and the footbridge, making a stop at the
waterfalls to observe an enormous juniper that could be in the
Colorado Historic Trees book.

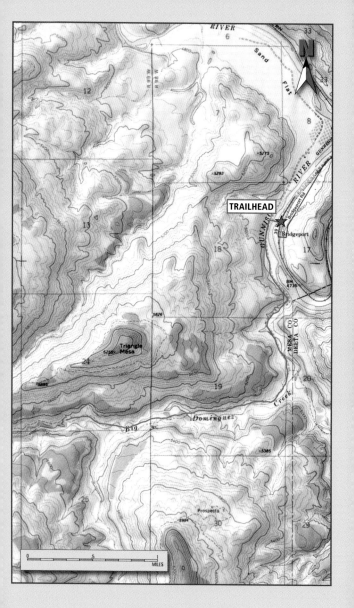

5. Fisher Towers

BY ROD MARTINEZ

MAPS	Trails Illustrated, Moab North, Number 500 USGS, Fisher Towers, 7.5 minute
ELEVATION GAIN	670 feet
RATING	Easy–moderate
ROUND-TRIP DISTANCE	4.6 miles
ROUND-TRIP TIME	4–5 hours
NEAREST LANDMARK	Hwy 128, in Utah

COMMENT: The Fisher Towers are an incredible feature along Utah's portion of the Colorado River. The rock pinnacles rise high above a maze of red and purple-hued canyons. Hikers and visitors will be treated to a panoramic view of Castle Rock, Richardson Amphitheatre—enclosed in a cliff—the Colorado River, and the La Sal Mountains, as well as the always-impressive Fisher Towers.

The tallest tower, the 900-foot-high Titan, was not climbed until 1962. Three Colorado climbers, sponsored by National Geographic, were the first to accomplish this difficult feat.

The rock comprising the towers is crumbly and makes for difficult climbing conditions. More recent developments in rock climbing equipment and techniques, however, have made ascents fairly common. It is recommended that only highly experienced climbers attempt to scale the Fisher Towers.

The towers contain layers of sedimentary rock in various shades of maroon, red-purple, and red-brown colors. The colors result from varying amounts of hematite, an iron oxide.

The piles of hardened mud and the colorful canyon system have afforded terrific backgrounds for at least 27 movies, including *Rio Grande* and *Against a Crooked Sky.*

You can also enjoy visiting Fisher Towers in the winter when the snow-capped La Sal Mountains showcase the strength and height of the towers.

The Titan—900 feet tall.
PHOTO BY ROD MARTINEZ

GETTING THERE: From Grand Junction, take I-70 west for 52 miles, to exit 204 in Utah. Take the frontage road for approximately 3 miles to Hwy 128. Proceed south on Hwy 128 for about 20 miles. You will see the Fisher Towers on your left and at the base of the La Sal Mountains.

The access road is near MM 21 on Hwy 128. Turn left onto this road and follow it for about 2.2 miles to the trailhead. Restroom facilities are available at the trailhead.

THE ROUTE: This is an easy route to follow as it is well marked with a wide path, cairns, rocks, and logs. Do pay attention to the location of the cairns, especially on the slickrock portions, as it is easy to deviate slightly from the trail. If you do temporarily lose the trail, look around for trail markers. You cannot go too far astray, as you will come to a cliff edge or begin scaling rocks not meant for the average hiker.

The trail is skillfully crafted so that it follows the natural

The Colorado River, flowing through Richardson Amphitheatre in eastern Utah.

contours of the canyon land. It winds across to the mesa south of the parking lot, ascends above one of the cleft canyons descending from the tall towers, and hugs the sheer tall walls of the towers themselves—which you will see as you look down over the cliff edges.

Parts of this trail are not for less-adventuresome folks or those who experience vertigo. If you are bringing children, be aware of the edges and their closeness to the dramatic and steep dropoffs.

Plan to stop many times to photograph and admire the spires, grotesque-looking rocks, bridges, and balanced rocks adorning all the canyons surrounding you. You may see rock climbers aspiring to reach the top of some of the pinnacles and truly brave and skilled adventurers striving for the top of the 900-foot-tall Titan.

Take time to enjoy the panoramic scenery at many points along the way. At the end of the trail, the view is breathtaking as you look to the south at the La Sal Mountains and Onion Creek, to the west at Castle Valley, or to the north at the Colorado River winding through the red rock country. The most spectacular view now is of the Titan, about 0.5 mile away and revealing its full 900-foot stature as the highest of the Fisher Towers.

As you turn around and head back to the parking area, you will get different and exciting views of the same rocks and towers you hiked along on your way in.

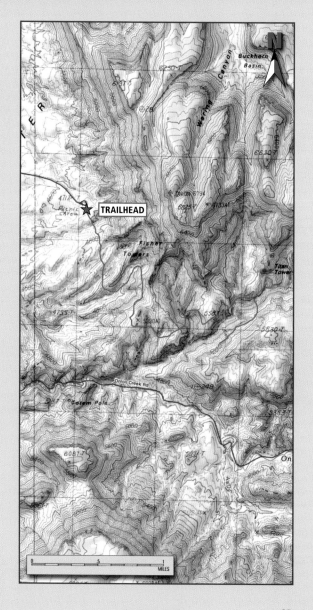

TRAILHEAD

6. Flume Canyon Trail

BY MARY McCUTCHAN

MAPS	Trails Illustrated, Grand Junction/Fruita, Number 502 USGS, Colorado National Monument, 7.5 minute
ELEVATION GAIN	250 feet gain/loss
RATING	Moderate
ROUND-TRIP DISTANCE	4.2 miles—a "balloon loop"
ROUND-TRIP TIME	4 hours
NEAREST LANDMARK	East entrance to Colorado National Monument

COMMENT: Flume Canyon is a delightful, moderate loop in the heart of McInnis Canyons National Conservation Area (NCA), taking you into the Black Ridge Wilderness and back out. Views of Entrada sandstone with its smooth slopes, hoodoos, and balanced rocks are a highlight. This is a versatile trailhead as you can combine with the Pollock Bench trail to create many different loop hikes or even take the longer hike to Rattlesnake Arches.

GETTING THERE: Go 17 miles from the Horizon Drive–I-70 interchange in Grand Junction to the Fruita exit. Take the Fruita exit south across the Colorado River to the Horsethief Bench turnoff, across from Dinosaur Hill. Turn right here and go through the Kingsview subdivision. Turn left on the gravel road, passing Devils Canyon, Opal Hill, and Fruita Paleo trailheads. Continue until you see the Pollock Bench trailhead, with a pit toilet on your left. There is a register and map box, but to be safe bring your own map. Dogs and equestrians are allowed, but please pick up after Fido.

THE ROUTE: Leave the trailhead, bearing to your left (going right takes you up the hill on Pollock Bench). Follow the most worn route down and across the Flume drainage, where it guides you south onto an old road. The trail soon leaves the road, turning right. You'll see a rehabilitated trail and also a "social" trail going

Sandstone castles along the trail to Flume Canyon.   PHOTO BY ROD MARTINEZ

to the left. The open social trail is okay, but a dead end, so continue trending right and south through the cacti and rabbit brush to the intersection of P2 and F1. (P2, going 0.2 mile west uphill, returns back to Pollock Bench.)

Follow F1 to the left, via rock cairns and across the sandy drainage, and the wider trail heading uphill. (To the left is a spur trail that reaches into the bottom of Flume Canyon itself.) Continue up the hill to a marked intersection for F1—the beginning of the loop part. Turn right for a counterclockwise circuit past some erosion-control wattles and into the Black Ridge Wilderness.

In about 15 minutes, you can look right, or west, to the Entrada formations. The trail will bring you close to eroded Entrada formations; stay alert here for the main path, as social trails could mislead you. Once you are about 1.8 miles along, you'll see a subtle drainage coming from the right and you will reach an intersection with another connector to Pollock. A little before this is a balanced rock to your right. This intersection can be confusing, so remember you want to stay on F1. (F2 connects

A balanced rock.

to Pollock trending west.) Bear left, continuing south, then east up a rise to a steep section leading back down into the main Flume drainage.

Turning back and crossing the seasonal stream, you are at the "head" of the canyon. Flume Canyon will gradually drop away and the trail will rise up some natural stone steps after you've made the turn and headed north back to the trailhead. Be sure to take advantage of views and overlooks early at this point because the trail leaves the canyon. About 1.0 mile from the F2-F1 intersection, after completing the "turn-around," there is an intersection with D1, leading over to the Devils Canyon trail system. Both areas are crisscrossed by a series of geologic faults. That is why you'll see Entrada stone up higher behind and beyond you in the distance.

Stay on F1 and enjoy winding about in the rock and sage as you gradually come up to the height you attained on the west side. You'll return to that same F1 intersection. A sign on the F1 road portion directs you to the correct trail leading across the drainage and back to the trailhead. Look for rabbits, Desert Bighorn Sheep, deer, and collared lizards.

7. Liberty Cap/Corkscrew/ Corkscrew Connector

BY CAROLYN EMANUEL

MAPS	Trails Illustrated, Grand Junction/Fruita Number 502 USGS, Colorado National Monument, 7.5 minute
ELEVATION GAIN	1,200 feet
RATING	Moderate
ROUND-TRIP DISTANCE	4.5 miles
ROUND-TRIP TIME	4 hours
NEAREST LANDMARK	East entrance to Colorado National Monument

COMMENT: This dramatic, geologically diverse trail begins in the Redlands, a subdivision of Grand Junction. It starts very near the Museum of Western Colorado's Riggs Hill, named for archeologist Elmer Riggs who unearthed a large dinosaur, Apatosaurus, here in 1903. Riggs Hill trail is a 1.0 mile, easy hike that features a myriad of historical and educational opportunities. If it were the 18th century, you could seek out Scotsman James Hutton as a hiking companion. Hutton brilliantly founded the science of geology and in so doing changed our understanding of the earth. Hutton would be wild about this hike. By the 19th century, geological history was divided into four great chunks of time, including the Precambrian that covers the dark rock you are now looking at. The Liberty Cap/Corkscrew/Corkscrew Connector trail takes you right through the earth's ages, most of which are Precambrian, or more than 500 million years old.

GETTING THERE: To access the trailhead from I-70, take 24 Road/ Redlands Parkway off I-70 West. Stay on Redlands Parkway past Riggs Hill. At Wildwood Road you need to take a right turn. Keep on Wildwood until you see a sign for Wildwood trailhead and parking lot. Turn into the parking area and take in the spectacular geology right in front of you. Begin your hike here.

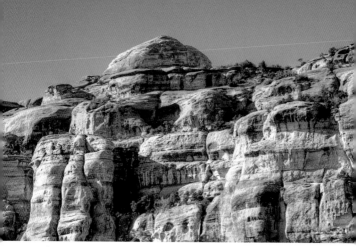

The top of the trail, resembling a "Liberty Cap." PHOTO BY ROD MARTINEZ

THE ROUTE: The trail begins at 4,800 feet elevation as it heads west for a mile, toward the dark black Precambrian rocks directly ahead. You will cross into a juniper, piñon pine, prickly pear, and sagebrush high-desert environment where, in the spring, the prickly pear are aflame with pink and yellow flowers. As you hike along the base of the Navajo and Wingate sandstone cliffs, you will begin to ascend a very well-constructed trail that switchbacks up through the Precambrian gneiss and schist. This new trail was completed in 2006. At places, the switchbacks give the hiker a tremendous view down into Precambrian granite and gneiss in a spectacular canyon. There are Jurassic-era boulders, some 208 million years old, strewn throughout this area.

Finally you top out on a Navajo sandstone bench, under towering Chinle and Wingate sandstone cliffs and monoliths, above the much older Precambrian formation.

Your hike eventually comes to a new trail sign indicating the Liberty Cap trailhead 0.5 mile ahead. You choose what your legs feel up to for the day. Go left and you ascend the very steep and rocky trail to the Liberty Cap, a memorable trail because it powers up through the Rock of Ages to the actual Cap itself, a sand dune frozen in time.

The trail twists and turns—hence its name.   PHOTO BY RICK EMANUEL

Ascend the final push to Liberty Cap, named after the hats worn by patriots in the Revolutionary War. There is some exposure in the final 300 feet, as you cross a sandstone ledge immediately before the Cap itself. After viewing the Cap up close, you might agree with Grand Valley mountaineer Seth Loki who said, "It looks like a Hershey's Kiss that refuses to melt."

If you wish to do more than sit at the base of the Cap and admire the spectacular views, you can climb the Cap on a 15-foot ladder on the back of the dome. The ladder was constructed by the Colorado National Monument's first superintendent, John Otto, and is a masterful example of his legendary, early 20th-century, trail-building style.

8. Main Canyon—Little Bookcliffs Wild Horse Area

BY JOHN GASCOYNE

MAPS	USGS, Cameo, 7.5 minute USGS, Round Mountain, 7.5 minute
ELEVATION GAIN	About 100 feet elevation loss to bottom of canyon
RATING	Easy–moderate
ROUND-TRIP DISTANCE	3 miles (farther if you choose)
ROUND-TRIP TIME	1.5 hours
NEAREST LANDMARK	Power plant at Cameo exit from I-70

COMMENT: Over breakfast in Grand Junction, it was suggested that we might encounter some wild horses on our proposed hike. Even the name of the hike, Little Bookcliffs Wild Horse Area, held promise. Although we are fairly serious Colorado hikers, none of us had ever had a personal face-off with a wild stallion or even so much as a free-roaming colt or filly.

Once on the trail things soon changed—dramatically. A large black stallion appeared on a hill above us. Three cameras began shooting. Two more horses appeared higher up, then more. Our excitement was almost palpable. Out of respect, however, we resisted the temptation to move in too closely.

There was more excitement left. As we began hiking back, we encountered two herds with five horses in each. Two horses, one from each group, decided to go a couple of rounds. The combat seemed more serious than just ritualistic—the fighters rose up off their front legs, slashing and biting. The fight didn't last long, however, and stopped suddenly with no apparent winner.

A note on wild horses: Different folks have different, thoughtful opinions on whether any horses in this country can truly be considered wild. Some observers see them as nonnative "feral" animals, destructive of grazing lands in competition with other species, both wild and domestic.

Other people point out that the genus *Equus*, the remote

A challenge between leaders of different herds.   PHOTO BY JOHN GASCOYNE

ancestor of all modern-day horses, roamed North America many thousands of years ago and that present-day wild horses, originally derived from the herds of Spanish explorers, should be regarded as a reintroduction and not as an invasive species. These folks find majesty and fascination in wild horse populations and want them protected and left free to roam.

Although there are many wild horse herds throughout the West, the Little Bookcliffs Wild Horse Area is one of only three sites that are reserved specifically for wild horses.

There is no guarantee that wild horses will always be viewable at this site. Early spring is the best time to find them at this lower elevation.

GETTING THERE: From Grand Junction, drive northeast on Interstate 70 and take the Cameo exit. Drive across the one-lane bridge, with the power plant on your left. You will be traveling on the Coal Canyon Road. This is a somewhat rough road and you will cross some drainages. If there is water in the road, exercise caution and look before trying to cross, especially in a passenger

Hikers in Main Canyon walking toward Grand Mesa.   PHOTO BY JOHN GASCOYNE

car. After about 1.5 miles, there will be a Y in the road; bear to
the right here and take the Main Canyon road a short distance to
the trailhead marked Little Bookcliffs Wild Horse Area. There are
no restrooms or other facilities at the trailhead.

THE ROUTE: Walk to the right of the trailhead sign, going uphill on a
dirt road, to a gate at the top of the short path. Proceed through
the gate, taking care to see that it is chained again after you go
through. Follow the roadway to your right and go downhill a
short way, to the bottom of the slope. There may be a cairn at
the bottom of the hill. Once there, make a hard left turn and you
will be in Main Canyon, on the occasionally marked trail, and
generally heading in a northwesterly direction. A stream meanders through this canyon and you will encounter a number of
water crossings, so exercise caution. In keeping with the
easy-moderate designation we have given this hike, it is
suggested that you turn around and retrace your path after
about 1.5 miles or 90 minutes. To extend the hike, you can stay
on the canyon floor and pass Spring Creek Canyon, on your left
after about a mile from the trailhead, and then continue about
4 more miles to the junction with Cottonwood Canyon—Main
Canyon continues to the right.

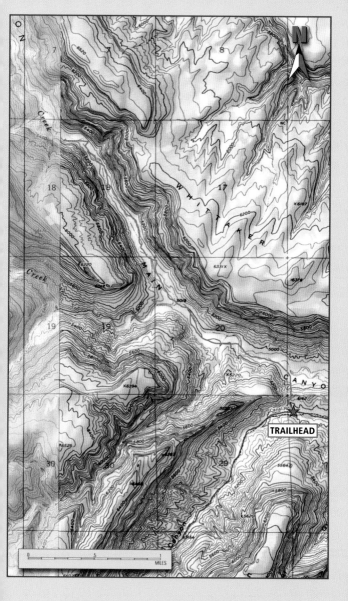

TRAILHEAD

9. Mica Mine Trail

BY CAROL BUTLER

MAPS	Trails Illustrated, Grand Junction/Fruita, Number 502 Glade Park and Island Mesa local maps
ELEVATION GAIN	150 feet
RATING	Easy
ROUND-TRIP DISTANCE	2.6 miles
ROUND-TRIP TIME	2–3 hours
NEAREST LANDMARK	Little Park Road

COMMENT: The Mica Mine trail is a popular local hike that takes you to the only mica mine in Mesa County. Mica occurs in a dome of Precambrian rocks—in a zoned pegmatite deposit with layers of feldspar, quartz, and muscovite mica.

Benton Canon was a banker and a leading citizen of Grand Junction in the 1880s and 1890s. He discovered the deposit of mica in Ladder Canyon prior to 1895. Sam A. Grady and three other men filed the first claim on the Ladder Canyon Prospect in 1907. The mine was named the White Rose Mica lode. Sam Grady worked the mine until 1926. It had to have been hard work to operate the mine and to carry the mica down to Grand Junction by mule and wagon.

From 1967 through 1976, the mine was under claim and quarried by brothers Vern and Willis Kelley and their Skyline Mining Company. From 1977 to 1987, Fred Montoya and his son and brother operated the quarry, mining decorative quartz. There has been no significant mining activity since 1987. The mine was never large and was probably only marginally profitable.

There are piles of white quartz in the canyon, and a hiker can find a hole in the canyon wall, about 40 feet north of the mine, where explosives were stored. There are some old timbers at the site, probably from a mine chute.

This trail is in a cool and shady canyon with a stream that flows in early spring and that can disappear entirely in July and

Desert varnish paints the sandstone wall.

August of dry years. Trees along the trail include cottonwood, Utah juniper, piñon pine, and wild mahogany. Springtime wildflowers include Indian paintbrush, evening primrose, larkspur, wallflower, and locoweed. The trail is suitable for children and dogs. Morning is the best time to hike.

GETTING THERE: From the corner of 1st Street and Grand Avenue in Grand Junction, travel west on Hwy 340 0.6 mile until reaching Monument Road and turn left. Drive 0.1 mile and turn left onto D Road (also known as Rosevale Road). Travel on D Road 1.2 miles to Little Park Road and turn right. Little Park Road is steep and twists for 5.2 miles until a large sign for Bangs Canyon is seen on the left. Turn left and park here. There are restrooms available, but no water.

THE ROUTE: Facing south at the parking lot, the Mica Mines trail is in front of you and heads off to the right. The trail follows an old wagon trail. You will quickly reach sandstone steps leading down into Rough Canyon. Turn right at the T intersection. Within 100 feet, there will be a first creek crossing. The trail will cross the creek, or a dry creek bed, many times, but it always remains close to the water or creek bed. Stay on the main trail. Ladder

A hole in the red sandstone wall
creates an arch formation.

Canyon can now be seen. After 0.5 mile, high cliffs to the right
show desert varnish. Note how the cliff has been eroded by
water.

At 0.75 mile, small pieces of quartz and mica are scattered
along the trail and bank sides. Close to 1.2 miles, you will cross
the creek on a log bridge. At 1.3 miles, take the path on the left to
the Mica Mine. There are many mica-studded boulders to climb
on here. As you face the quarry, look overhead at the large mica
crystal imbedded in rose quartz.

If you continue 0.2 mile past the mine, you will reach a
waterfall and a nice lunch stop. This is a rougher and steeper
stretch and is not suitable for small children. Retrace your steps
to the trailhead.

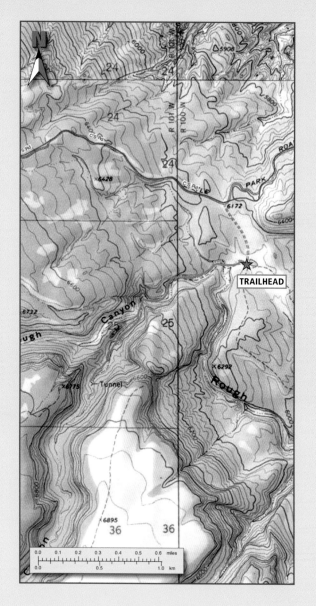

TRAILHEAD

10. Monument Canyon Trail

BY ROD MARTINEZ

MAPS	Trails Illustrated, Grand Junction/Fruita, Number 502 USGS, Colorado National Monument, 7.5 minute
ELEVATION GAIN	About 747 feet elevation loss to bottom of canyon
RATING	Easy–moderate
ROUND-TRIP DISTANCE	12 miles—recommend a car shuttle at lower trailhead for a one-way hike of 6 miles
ROUND-TRIP TIME	7–8 hours or 3.5–4 hours with car shuttle
NEAREST LANDMARK	Colorado National Monument Visitor Center

COMMENT: The Monument Canyon trail offers a spectacular hike through the heart of the Colorado National Monument (CNM). The CNM is located on the northwest corner of the Colorado Plateau, a semidesert land featuring Utah junipers, piñon pine, a variety of cacti, and abundant wildflowers. Look for squirrels, lizards, mule deer, coyotes, and the ever-elusive Desert Bighorn Sheep. The 23 mile Rim Rock Drive, taken by most visitors, has numerous turnouts and short hikes to view the many sheer-walled canyons and amazing rock formations and spires, such as Squaw Fingers, Kissing Couple, and the much-photographed Independence Monument.

To really embrace the beauty and ruggedness of the CNM, you must leave your vehicle and hike any one of the 14 trails, some of which are described elsewhere in this guide. The heart of the CNM, however, can best be explored via the Monument Canyon trail.

GETTING THERE: From Interstate 70, take Fruita exit 19 and head south toward the redrock formation. It is 2.4 miles to the CNM west entrance. Here you need to make a decision: do a car shuttle, which will result in a 6.0 mile hike from the upper trailhead, or start at the lower trailhead—2.1 miles southeast of the entrance—for a 12 mile roundtrip hike. It is highly

Independence Monument rises 450 feet above the trail.   PHOTO BY ROD MARTINEZ

recommended to do the car shuttle, leaving one car at the bottom, then driving 8.0 miles from the entrance to the upper trailhead and beginning from there.

THE ROUTE: From the upper trailhead, you will begin a rapid descent of 747 feet in slightly less than 1.0 mile. Although the trail is well maintained, it is steep and rocky in places. About 300 yards down the trail you will come to a junction with the Coke Ovens trail, which will take you to the base of the rock formations that resemble coke ovens. This side trail is not described here.

As you descend, observe the 500-foot-high red sandstone walls as they rise above you. There are a few large alcoves that, in geologic time, may succumb to wind and water erosion to become stone arches. When the trail reaches the bottom, you will cross a small stream that flows only in late winter and early spring. Spring also brings out a vast array of wildflowers and an abundance of cacti that will be in full blossom during the first two weeks of June.

Looking from the top into Monument Canyon
with the Coke Oven formations on the right.

While traversing the trail, you will be shaded by piñon pine
and juniper trees. After 1.8 miles, turn left and begin following
the walls of Monument Canyon. As the canyon opens up, you will
begin to pass by the giant redrock formations that give Monument Canyon its name. These include Pipe Organ, Praying
Hands, Kissing Couple, and the celebrated Independence
Monument. At 3.5 miles, you will be at the base of the 450-foot-
tall Independence Monument, the largest freestanding rock
formation in the CNM.

Follow the trail through the cacti, as it winds its way down
and along the canyon wall, before you take another left turn to
follow the fence line to the lower trailhead. If you do this hike
early in the day during the fall you will have a great chance to
observe mule deer, coyotes, and a herd of Desert Bighorn Sheep.
If this is a round-trip hike, turn around here and hike back 6.0
miles and ascend 747 feet to where you began. Otherwise, get in
your car and enjoy the drive back to your other vehicle at the
upper trailhead.

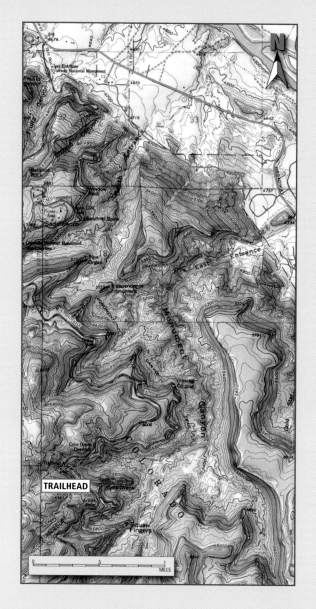

TRAILHEAD

11. Mount Garfield

BY DAVID HANLEY

MAPS	Trails Illustrated, Colorado National Monument/McInnis Canyons NCA, Number 208 USGS, Round Mountain/Clifton, 7.5 minute Latitude 40, Durango Trails
ELEVATION GAIN	2,000 feet
RATING	Difficult
ROUND-TRIP DISTANCE	4.0 miles
ROUND-TRIP TIME	2.5–4 hours
NEAREST LANDMARK	I-70, Town of Palisade

COMMENT: At the east end of the Grand Valley, Mount Garfield stands tall as one of the most prominent geographical and geological features of the Grand Junction area. Its summit is the highest point in the Bookcliffs formation—a nearly 200-mile-long band of sedimentary cliffs, extending from Palisade, Colorado, to Price Canyon, Utah. This hike is one of the real classics in our area.

The route to the summit is a steep 2.0 mile, 2,000-foot ascent from the valley floor and winding up through layers of Mancos shale and Mesa Verde limestone. This hike will challenge both your legs and your lungs. Your reward is the incredible 360-degree views from the summit—including the Grand Valley, Grand Mesa, Bookcliffs, and even farther. Besides the views, lucky hikers may have a chance to see some of the wild horses who reside in this area, as well as many other wild desert inhabitants.

While not the longest hike in the area, the combination of steep slopes, exposed terrain, and unstable footing render this hike one of the most difficult in the region, an adventure not to be taken lightly. Bring plenty of water, at least 3 quarts, and do not attempt the hike if the trail is wet or icy.

GETTING THERE: From Interstate 70, take exit 42 (at the town of Palisade), head south on 37 3/10 Road for 0.15 mile and turn

Late light on Mount Garfield.

right onto G 7/10 Road. Follow this road for approximately 1.0 mile west and then to the north 0.6 mile, where you will pass through a narrow tunnel under I-70. The parking area and trailhead are clearly marked on the north side of the interstate.

THE ROUTE: From the parking area, follow the well-marked trail a short distance to the northwest, to the base of a steep ridge that climbs northward. From here, the trail ascends this very steep and narrow shale ridge approximately 600 vertical feet. The shale can make for some slippery footing, so step carefully and do not attempt this hike if the trail is wet.

The initial climb up the ridge will give way to a moderate scramble up another 200 feet to a small terrace. This is a good spot to catch your breath and enjoy the views of the valley and the steep portion you have just hiked. Look up the slope to the northeast for a good view of the old Gearhart mine.

From here, continue up the trail through another short, moderate scramble, up to a larger bench. This bench marks the halfway point of the hike and provides a quiet and gentle walk through the piñon/juniper woodland. It is a good spot to take a break before beginning the final push to the top.

At the top, looking at the Bookcliff Mountain Range.   PHOTO BY DAVID HANLEY

From the bench, the trail heads west up another steep climb along the base of the sandstone cliffs to a prominent saddle. This section of the trail to the saddle is perhaps the most exciting— and the most treacherous—part of the hike due to exposed trail sections with significant drop-offs. Hike carefully through here and take your time to enjoy the impressive terrain both above and below you. Soon after you pass along the base of the large cliffs, you will arrive at the saddle and the home stretch of the hike.

From the saddle, continue west on the trail, up through a moderate sandstone slope to the final ridgeline. Once you are on the ridge, it is an easy 0.25 mile hike to the summit, at 6,765 feet. The summit is clearly marked with a USGS benchmark and the remains of a flagpole. From the summit you will be treated to magnificent views in all directions.

Use caution as you retrace your steps to the trailhead. Due to the loose and often slippery footing, the steep descent can prove more challenging than the ascent—plan to take at least one hour to get back to the trailhead.

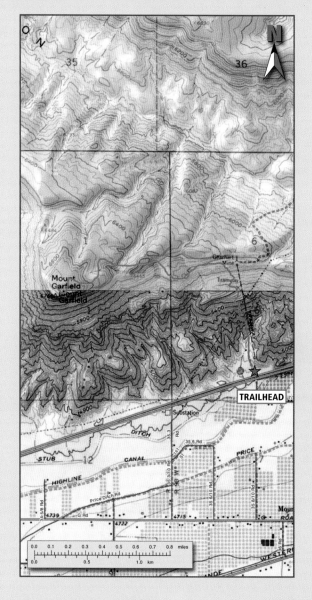

TRAILHEAD

12. No Thoroughfare Canyon (NTC)

BY ALLAN CONRAD

MAPS	Trails Illustrated, Grand Junction/Fruita, Number 502 USGS, Colorado National Monument, 7.5 minute
ELEVATION GAIN	700 feet
RATING	Moderate
ROUND-TRIP DISTANCE	6 miles
ROUND-TRIP TIME	5 hours
NEAREST LANDMARK	East entrance, Colorado National Monument

COMMENT: It may seem amazing that you can find waterfalls just outside of Grand Junction, but you can. Of the many hikes in the Colorado National Monument (CNM), this hike is a gem for folks seeking a hike that's straightforward but with a more rugged feel to it than you'll find on a standard trail. And, families can do the hike with children who have some trail experience. This route appeals to many: I saw two young mothers with their daughters at the first pool, at about mile 1.0, and a couple of gung-ho backpackers headed for the unmaintained region above the second waterfall.

Precambrian rock lies below the red sandstone formations of the Colorado National Monument. You'll be following the Precambrian streambed most of the day. As you work your way around and above waterfalls, there will be some steep sections through broken terrain. Depending on the season, the flows are most apt to be modest. During periods of rain, however, you are advised not to spend time near the streambed: there is evidence of flash flooding and high runoff in the canyon.

GETTING THERE: From the Grand Avenue, 1st Street, Hwy 50, and Hwy 340 intersection in Grand Junction, proceed west on 340 for 0.9 mile to Monument Road. Make a left-hand turn at the traffic light to go to the Colorado National Monument. The entrance station is 3.4 miles south of Hwy 340. Entrance fees of

Initial stream crossing in No Thoroughfare Canyon.   PHOTO BY ALLAN CONRAD

$10 per vehicle apply. The Devil's Kitchen trailhead parking is on the left, 0.25 mile beyond the entrance station. Park here.

THE ROUTE: As you descend to the streambed on a wide path, stay to the right at the subsequent Ys. When you reach the streambed at 0.4 mile—where a carsonite sign and cairn existed as of April 2011—look around. Aim for the path 50 yards to the right on the other side of the stream; ignore the path immediately opposite your position.

The route for this hike goes along the streambed, except for the steep ascent where the path will go right, around the waterfalls. The trail is not developed and requires some route finding from time to time. The well-traveled route follows a path that is sometimes on one side of the streambed and sometimes on the other. Most stream crossings have strategically placed step-across stones. Traveling up the canyon will take you from the wider portions into the narrower ones, where the stream bottom gets congested. At some places, there are short sections of slanted rock "benches," just above water level, that, with care, can be traversed. Depending on a hiker's experience, this rock scampering may be the toughest portion of this hike.

As you approach the water attractions, there will be more boulders in your path and you'll need to step between them. There is no specified trail in this part. It's best to proceed up

First waterfall in NTC.

canyon by working toward the right side of the canyon. Problems in negotiating your way are more pronounced as you near the first waterfall. This, along with the steep passage around the formation above the first waterfall, and increased rock scampering, warrant a "moderate" designation for this part of the hike.

At the base of the first waterfall, mile 1.8, a sign advises "Unmaintained route beyond this point!" The route finding in this first section, leading to the second waterfall, is a bit more demanding, but the narrow canyon bottom will guide your path forward. In about a mile, you'll be working through some boulders as you approach some steep cliffs on the left. Up ahead, you'll see the tallest waterfall in the canyon. Depending upon the time of year, its flow may seem meager or fairly strong.

Proceeding up the hill to the right would put you on a path toward the upper trailhead. That portion of NTC is a great scenic hike, but, due to the terrain and route-finding challenges, should be attempted only by experienced hikers. This extension of the hike is not described here; do your homework before attempting it.

Retrace your steps to return to the trailhead.

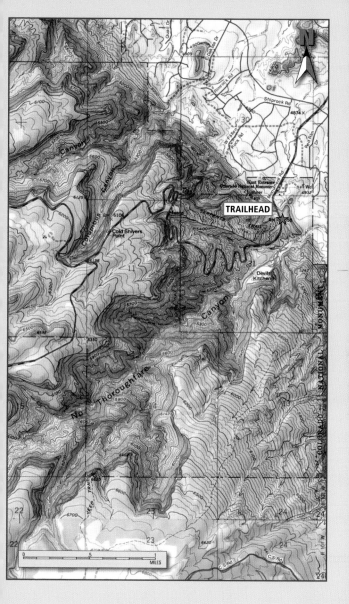

13. Rabbit Ears Trail

BY CAROL BUTLER

MAPS	Trails Illustrated, Grand Junction/Fruita, Number 502 USGS, Bitter Creek Well, UT/CO, 7.5 minute
ELEVATION GAIN	700 feet
RATING	Moderate
ROUND-TRIP DISTANCE	6.2 miles
ROUND-TRIP TIME	3–4 hours
NEAREST LANDMARK	I-70, exit 2

COMMENT: The Rabbit Ears Trail offers a pleasant hike in the high Colorado desert, with outstanding views of the Colorado River in Ruby Canyon and canyons of the McInnis Canyons National Conservation Area (NCA). You also will enjoy great views across the Grand Valley to the Bookcliffs. Utah juniper is the most common tree here. There are smaller numbers of piñon pine, wild mahogany, shadscale, yucca, Mormon tea, and rabbit bush. Indian paintbrush, globe mallow, Texas blueweed, prince's plum, and snakeweed are commonly seen in the spring. The hike leads to the top of Rabbit Ear mesa and then circles the perimeter of the mesa, affording excellent views of the surrounding territory.

The best time to hike Rabbit Ears Trail is spring, fall, or winter. In summer, you should start early in the day to avoid the worst heat. The trail may not be suitable in wet weather.

GETTING THERE: From Grand Junction, go west on I-70 to exit 2, for Rabbit Valley. Turn left and drive over the overpass to a cattle guard. Zero out your trip odometer here. From the cattle guard, drive 0.2 mile to a large sign and turn left onto an improved gravel road. Go 0.2 mile farther down the road, where there are restrooms located to the left. Continue east on the gravel road (which parallels I-70). At 1.9 miles there is an old corral on the right side of the road. You will cross another cattle guard at 4.4 miles. The parking lot and trailhead sign are at 4.5 miles.

A long and winding trail.

PHOTO BY CAROL BUTLER

THE ROUTE: The trail is generally composed of outcrops of sandstone, mixed with small rocks and gravel. The Bookcliffs are
visible to the north and Grand Mesa can be seen to the east. For
the first 0.3 mile, the trail is moderately steep until it reaches a
ridge. Walk along the ridgetop to your left. After 1.0 mile, there is
a rocky section of trail and then a narrow slot through the rock.
At about 1.2 miles, you will reach a small saddle and get your
first glimpse of the Colorado River. At the saddle, a cairn marks a
split in the trail. Take the left fork in the trail and begin the loop
that will travel clockwise around and up the mesa.

It is a steep climb to the mesa top. You will reach the top
about 1.5 miles from the trailhead. At 2.0 miles, the trail turns
west and proceeds for about 1.1 miles along the south edge of
the mesa. Stay alert, as the trail is faint in places and not well
marked by cairns. The trail is never far from the mesa edge,
which will always be on your left. There are many places to stop
and view the Colorado River in Ruby Canyon, the rugged canyon
country across the river, and, on a clear day, the La Sal
Mountains.

A captivating view of the Bookcliff Mountain range. PHOTO BY CAROL BUTLER

About 3.1 miles into the hike the southwest corner of Rabbit Ears Mesa is reached and the trail heads back to the north/northeast. Mee Canyon is the large canyon coming into Ruby Canyon on the far side of the river.

At 3.6 miles, the trail reaches the north edge of the mesa and the views are quite different. The Bookcliffs are visible in the distance, as is the dry desert country west of the Grand Valley. The trail begins to descend at 4.4 miles, and a series of switchbacks begins at 4.7 miles. Stay left at the junction of two small trails in this area. The trail is mostly downhill as it heads back to the saddle where it had split. The trail junction ending the loop section is at 5.0 miles. Retrace the last 1.2 miles of the trail back to the trailhead.

CRYPTOBIOTIC SOIL

This term describes very fragile soil crusts commonly found in the desert country. This crust is comprised of soil cyanobacteria, lichens, and mosses that play an important ecological role. In the cold deserts of the Colorado Plateau region—parts of Colorado, Utah, Arizona, and New Mexico—these crusts are very old and very well developed, often representing more than 70 percent of the living ground cover.

Cryptobiotic crusts increase the stability of otherwise easily eroded soils and increase fertility in soils often lacking such essential nutrients as nitrogen and carbon. These soil crusts are highly susceptible to soil-surface disturbance such as trampling by feet, hooves, or off-road vehicles.

We can all respect the red rock country and preserve it for future generations by staying on designated trails and avoiding any walking on these important and fragile soils.

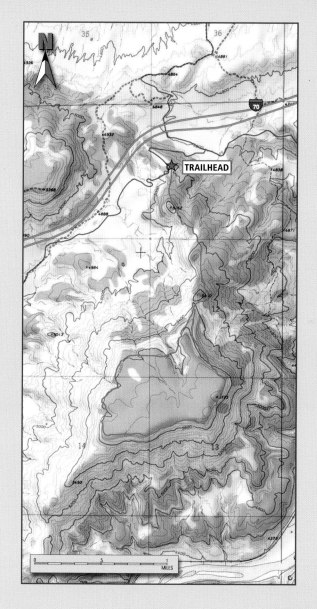

TRAILHEAD

14. Rattlesnake Canyon

BY ROD MARTINEZ

MAPS	Trails Illustrated, Grand Junction/Fruita, Number 502 USGS, Battleship Rock/Mack, 7.5 minute
ELEVATION GAIN	2,500 feet
RATING	Difficult–strenuous
ROUND-TRIP DISTANCE	14.2 miles
ROUND-TRIP TIME	8–10 hours
NEAREST LANDMARK	I-70, exit 19

COMMENT: Rattlesnake Canyon is in the Black Ridge Canyons Wilderness Area that forms the scenic heart of the McInnis Canyons National Conservation Area (NCA). The ledge on the eastern side of Rattlesnake Canyon contains 9 arches—the second-largest concentration outside of Arches National Park. These openings in the sandstone were created by a combination of wind and water.

The last arch, at the southern end of the canyon, is called Cedar Tree Arch, because of the large cedar tree growing beside it, or Rainbow Arch, because of its shape. With some effort, a good deal of skill, and minimal climbing equipment you can ascend through this arch to the top of the cliff. Once at the top, a half-mile hike will take you back to the trailhead for the 4x4 road. I recommend you try this hike and climb at another time.

Some of the arches are truly unique. Cedar Tree Arch has a span of 76 feet and an opening height of 43 feet. Bridge Arch, also known as Hole-in-the-Bridge Arch because of the opening dead center in the arch, has a span of 40 feet and an opening of 30 feet. My personal favorite is East Rim Arch, also known as Akiti Arch or Centennial Arch. It also has a span of 40 feet, but an opening height of 120 feet. The other 6 arches have similar openings and heights. This area is considered the gem of the McInnis Canyons NCA.

GETTING THERE: There are three different ways to access Rattlesnake Canyon and its 9 arches. One way, not recommended, is to

Cedar Tree, a/k/a Rainbow, Arch.   PHOTO BY ROD MARTINEZ

float the Colorado River from the Loma boat launch to the
mouth of Rattlesnake Canyon. The hike to the level where the
arches are located is a steep and strenuous game trail.

The second way, in some respects easiest, is to drive about
13 miles one way on a series of dirt roads. This requires a high-

Eye Arch.

PHOTO BY ROD MARTINEZ

clearance four-wheel-drive vehicle, and the road is closed from mid-November to mid-April. Due to steep and rocky grades, these roads should be attempted only under dry conditions. Driving in will shorten the hike by about 9 miles.

To do the hike we describe: from Grand Junction take I-70 west to exit 19, the Fruita exit. Head south and go 1.5 miles to Kingsview Estates. Turn right, into the subdivision, staying on the main road until it becomes a dirt road. The Pollock Bench trailhead is approximately 6 miles from the beginning of the dirt road, on the left side of the road.

THE ROUTE: The trail begins at the Pollock Bench trailhead. It is wide for the first 0.1 mile, until you reach a fork that can lead to Flume Canyon. Stay right and head west. After another 1.6 miles, you will intersect with trail R-1; leave trail P-1 (which you are on) and take R-1 to Rattlesnake Canyon and the arches. You will gain a substantial amount of elevation as the trail goes up over ridges and cliffs. This will be lost again as the trail descends into gullies and canyons.

This ever-changing terrain will wear on your legs, but the changes in geology will offer a great variety of rock formations and views. At about 2.4 miles, the trail descends a cliff that will require using your hands for balance as you scramble down the rocky trail. There is little or no exposure, but it does add a bit of adventure.

At 3.25 miles, you will encounter another cliff section that will require an upward scramble. Once on the top the trail heads mostly to the west. About 0.25 mile to your left you can see Window Rock Tower, containing an arch said to resemble South America. Farther to your left, about 0.5 mile away and along the rim of the canyon, you can hike to West Pollock Canyon Arch. This large arch is rarely explored. This could be a great side trip, although there is no distinct trail to the arch.

Sego lilies.

PHOTO BY ROD MARTINEZ

Bridge Arch.

At about 0.5 mile past where you see Window Rock Tower, the trail will intersect with a trail that can take you to the top of the ridge of this canyon ledge and to the 4x4 road described in the Getting There section.

Stay right and continue west toward Rattlesnake Canyon. After another mile, you will go around the cliff and then begin heading south. You are now on the rim of the east side of Rattlesnake Canyon. After about another 0.25 mile, on your left you will begin to see the first of the 9 arches. As you hike to the end of the canyon, be sure to take the short side trails so you can see each of the different arches. Cedar Tree (Rainbow) Arch is at the end of the canyon. Contemplate the beauty of this hike, then head back the same way you came in.

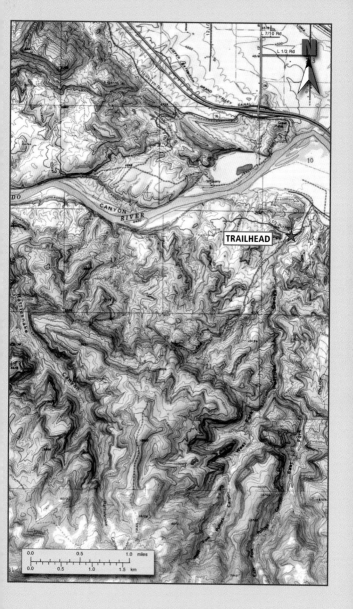

TRAILHEAD

15. Serpents Trail

BY LON CARPENTER

MAPS	Trails Illustrated, Grand Junction/Fruita, Number 502
	USGS, Colorado National Monument, 7.5 minute
ELEVATION GAIN	770 feet
RATING	Moderate—because of elevation gain
ROUND-TRIP DISTANCE	3.5 miles
ROUND-TRIP TIME	1.25–1.50 hours
NEAREST LANDMARK	Colorado National Monument

COMMENT: Serpents Trail originally was a road from Grand Junction to the Glade Park area. In 1950, Rim Rock Drive was built on the upper portion of the Colorado National Monument (CNM). This left a 1.75 mile section of the former road as a great hiking trail. In the early days of automobile travel, the road was even steeper and narrower than it is today.

Serpents Trail was specifically designed to optimize the scenery of the park and it reflects engineering techniques used in the construction of early automobile roads in difficult terrain. John Otto, the original booster of the park's scenic wonders and the custodian of Colorado National Monument from 1911 to 1927, designed the original route of the road and was involved in its sporadic construction. The project also provided access to the Glade Park region, and local engineers and other citizens contributed to both its funding and its construction.

Serpents Trail now serves solely as a 1.75 mile foot trail, and the old dirt road loops among gigantic fallen boulders. Pause to admire the many balanced rocks and spectacular views of No Thoroughfare Canyon and the Grand Valley. As the trail gains elevation, more of the panoramic vistas of the Grand Valley are visible to the east, while outstanding towering red rock cliffs and canyons can be seen to the west. It was a difficult road for cars, but the trail, with the exception of the elevation gain, is an easy one for hikers.

Great canyon views on the east side
of the Colorado National Monument.

GETTING THERE: From the Grand Avenue, 1st Street, Hwy 50, and
Hwy 340 intersection in downtown Grand Junction, proceed
west on Hwy 340 for 0.9 mile to Monument Road. Make a left
turn at the traffic light to go to the Colorado National Monument. The entrance station is 3.4 miles south on Hwy 340. The
trailhead is located just inside of the east entrance of the CNM.
An entrance fee of $10.00 is required for each passenger vehicle.

There is limited parking, for 12 vehicles, at the lower trailhead
and overflow parking available at the Devil's Kitchen parking
area just north of the trailhead. You will also see a road to a
picnic area on your right, with an additional parking area.

THE ROUTE: This trail is simple and very easy to follow as it winds
through the Windgate sandstone formation, with 20 switchbacks.
You will reach the east end of the automobile tunnel on Rim
Rock Drive. Turn around here and "coast" back downhill to your

It's hard to count all the twists and turns.
PHOTO BY LON CARPENTER

vehicle. If you leave early in the morning, you can avoid most of the hikers who use the trail as a great way of staying in shape.

In the spring you will also have the best chance of observing some of the many animals and birds that live in the park. These include Desert Bighorn Sheep, deer, mountain lions, hawks, golden eagles, canyon wrens, and packrats. The Serpents Trail may be the "crookedest" trail in the Colorado National Monument, but it offers a great way to capture the essence of the Monument.

RED ROCK COUNTRY HIKING TIPS

BOOTS. Wear sturdy hiking boots with good tread. Many of the trails in red rock country have loose rock and are steep in some sections. Good boots will support your ankles and will help avoid slipping and falling.

WATER. This pack guide provides a number of water guidelines to follow while hiking. Bring more water than is recommended for most mountain hikes. This country often has higher temperatures. Have more water in your vehicle than you intend to carry on your hike. Hydrate well, before you hit the trail.

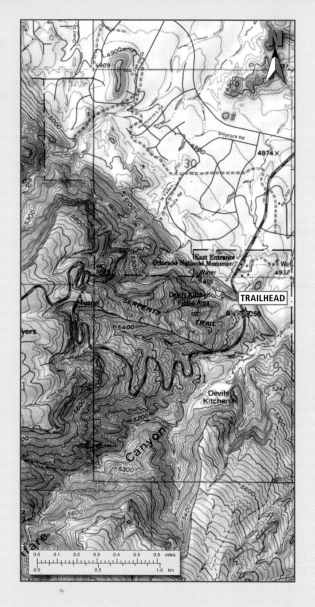

16. Spanish Trail/ Gunnison Bluffs

BY ROD MARTINEZ

MAPS	Trails Illustrated, Grand Junction/Fruita, Number 502 USGS, Grand Junction/Clifton/Whitewater, 7.5 minute
ELEVATION GAIN	1,150 feet
RATING	Easy–moderate (distance)
ROUND-TRIP DISTANCE	14 miles
ROUND-TRIP TIME	8–10 hours
NEAREST LANDMARK	Highway 50

COMMENT: Hiking the Spanish Trail will let you walk in the footsteps of Spanish explorers on their way to New Mexico or California. The trail is wide and easy to follow, with a few ravines. Spring and fall are the best seasons for this hike, but it can be done at any time. Summer can be rather hot and winter can be rather cool, especially if a breeze is stirring. The trail is hilly and you will continually gain and lose elevation as you follow the ruts carved by the Spanish explorers.

The Spanish Trail intersects with the Gunnison Bluffs Trail, which allows a number of combinations of the two. These combinations can range from an easy to a moderate hike of 8 to 10 miles, to a more difficult hike of 15 to 16 miles. This hike could be rated as difficult, but only because of its length. The beauty of the longer hike occurs where the trail travels along the cliffs of the Gunnison River. The trail is on the high desert, which is a stark contrast to the corridor of the Gunnison River, where cottonwood trees, grass, and wildlife abound. The river bottom has a train track following it from Delta to Grand Junction. Red rock cliffs and an environment of scrub brush, junipers, and other flora are part of the view across the Gunnison River that is not evident on the east side of the Gunnison— where the Gunnison Bluffs/Spanish Trail is located. Views to the east offer a terrific view of Mount Garfield and the Grand Mesa.

Gunnison bluffs and cliffs follow the Gunnison River. PHOTO BY ROD MARTINEZ

GETTING THERE: From downtown Grand Junction, take Hwy 50 south for 3.3 miles to 28 ½ Road. Make a right turn (south) onto 28 ½ Road, then make an immediate left (southeast) onto B Road, and then another immediate right just before you intersect with 28 ½ Road again. Park at the Gunnison Bluffs/Spanish Trail trailhead.

THE ROUTE: From the Gunnison Bluffs/Spanish Trail trailhead you will wind your way through a residential area. From the large parking area, walk southwest through an alley to Valley View Drive. Turn left onto Sunlight Drive, where it now turns into the trail. As you start the hike and descend the first of many hills, stay between the private property fence lines.

After you ascend a long, moderately steep hill you will make your first decision on where to continue your hike. After 1.1 miles the intersection with the Gunnison Bluffs trail is on your right and this trail will take you to the Gunnison cliffs. Take a right at this point and hike toward a large cellphone tower and to the edge of the cliffs above the Gunnison River. Follow the trail for 0.75 mile to the west, where it then turns and heads southwest and descends some bluffs and the wall of a canyon. The trail ascends back to the top of the bluffs, then heads east

A view of the Grand Mesa
as the Spanish Trail heads south.

for about 0.5 mile, where you will once again intersect with the Spanish Trail.

The trails stay together for about 0.1 mile, then separate, with the Spanish Trail going to the south and the Gunnison Bluffs trail going to the right. Continue to the right, or southwest, back to the cliffs above the Gunnison River. The trail is easy to follow, but always be aware of the location and direction of the carsonite signs that mark the trail and the direction you need to hike. There are numerous old four-wheel-drive roads and unused dirt bike and ATV trails. Being aware of and following these marker signs will keep you on the right path.

After about 4 miles from this intersection you will arrive at another large trailhead, which could be the starting point of this hike if started from the south end. This is also a great place to use a car shuttle if you want to limit the hike to 8–10 miles. Otherwise, you need to turn around and head back to the other trailhead by hiking the Spanish Trail directly back to your car. There are numerous hills and valleys, but it is a relatively easy 9 mile return.

Somewhere on your return, stop and close your eyes and use your imagination to wonder how this adventure would differ if you took this hike 150 years ago when the Spanish explorers used the trail.

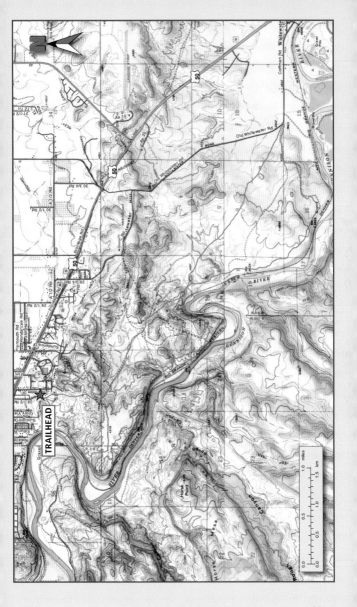

TRAILHEAD

17. Tellerico Trail to Corcoran Point

BY ALLAN CONRAD AND JOYCE FROST

MAPS	USGS, Corcoran Point, 7.5 minute
ELEVATION GAIN	2,800 feet
RATING	Moderate–difficult
ROUND-TRIP DISTANCE	6 miles (not including distance on Ute Trail)
ROUND-TRIP TIME	5 hours
NEAREST LANDMARK	Overpass of I-70 at 25 Road

COMMENT: The Bookcliffs are a prominent geologic feature of Western Colorado and Eastern Utah. The Little Bookcliffs Wild Horse Area, managed by the Bureau of Land Management (BLM), is on the plateaus atop the Bookcliffs, north of the Grand Junction Regional Airport. The Tellerico Trail ascends the rugged face of the Bookcliffs and provides a scenic pedestrian access to this plateau region.

As you ascend steeply above the changing views of the desert terrain—through the strata of sandstone and shale—what appeared from the distance to be a drab scene now becomes a spectacular display of flora, particularly in the spring, and fascinating geology.

The most hoped for fauna—the wild horses—may or may not be in view the day you hike, but you may see lizards, rabbits, or Gambel's quail.

Once the trail reaches the ridge west of Corcoran Point, the vistas of the face of the Bookcliffs, looking northwest and across the top of the Bookcliffs to Corcoran Peak to the north, come into view. You may choose to turn around at this point or you can turn easterly to climb 7,352-foot Corcoran Point, which is more than 500 feet higher than Mount Garfield. You can also continue to the intersection with the Ute Trail, thus gaining access to the trail network atop the Bookcliffs.

The BLM office can provide a brochure depicting this trail

Summit view toward the Grand Mesa and Mount Garfield.

PHOTO BY ALLAN CONRAD

network and they can also advise of travel conditions—the access road and the trail are truly unpleasant when the ground is wet.

GETTING THERE: From the intersection of 25 Road and Patterson Road, proceed north on 25 Road for 10.7 miles to a large, informal parking area near the mouth of a canyon at the base of the Bookcliffs. The road makes a turn at the 4 mile mark, followed in 0.25 mile by a bridge over the Government Highline Canal and the end of the paved roadway. The dirt and gravel road, rutted in places, continues in a northeasterly direction across the desert to a parking area on the right. Unfortunately, this site is usually trashy. Consider bringing a garbage bag along with you and carrying some of this trash out when you leave. (Hikers with short-wheel-based vehicles might choose to drive a few tenths of a mile farther up the canyon and park in one of the several turnouts.)

THE ROUTE: From the parking area, follow the roadway for 0.3 mile, going past some green metal posts that will lead you to the drainage, which turns left. The crux turn is the one out of the northeast-headed drainage, where you need to turn hard left at a carsonite sign and proceed up a slight grade. Follow the subsequent drainage a short distance until you come to a Y; stay left and start ascending steeply uphill. The trail drops down several

Interesting stratified geology.

times as it traverses from ridge to ridge across gullies before coming to the shoulder, west of and 500 feet below Corcoran Point.

If you wish to hike farther to the Ute Trail and/or to Corcoran Point, follow the trail to the right, where it steeply ascends 400 feet through loose soil, on some switchbacks, before leveling out in a piñon and juniper forest. Several social trails head to the right, toward Corcoran Point. Choose some likely looking path to the sandy summit area, which offers a scenic spot for lunch among the trees and views far across the Grand Valley.

From the point where the social trails leave the main trail, it is less than a 10-minute hike over gentle terrain to the intersection with the Ute Trail. Taking a right and going in the direction of Indian Park, there is a BLM sign about 30 yards past the intersection of Ute Trail and Tellerico Trail. If time allows, you could walk out and back a bit: left toward the North Soda Cabin, or right toward Indian Peak—where wild horses may be seen. Retrace your steps to return to the trailhead.

RED ROCK COUNTRY HIKING TIP

WEATHER. Wet weather will create muddy, slippery trails on Tellerico and Mt. Garfield. This can be a hazard on any of the red rock trails.

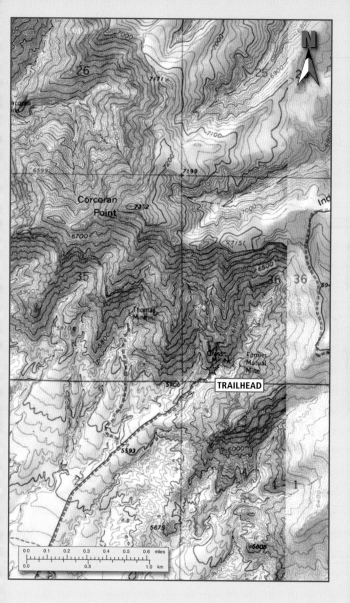

TRAILHEAD

18. Trail Through Time

BY LARRY ALLISON

MAPS	USGS, Bitter Creek Well, 7.5 minute
ELEVATION GAIN	160 feet
RATING	Easy
ROUND-TRIP DISTANCE	1.5 miles
ROUND-TRIP TIME	1.5–2 hours
NEAREST LANDMARK	I-70, exit 2

COMMENT: The Trail Through Time, in Rabbit Valley, is part of the Dinosaur Triangle and provides a wonderful introduction to the Jurassic Period geology and paleontology of Western Colorado and Eastern Utah. This is an interpretive trail that travels through the Morrison Formation—an important geological feature in the Grand Junction area—which provides rich and colorful bedding for many dinosaur fossils.

This trail is readily accessible from I-70, either by heading west toward Utah or by entering into Colorado from the west. The trail offers an easy, family-friendly hike. It introduces curious minds to dinosaur bones in situ and geologic processes, and features historical mining markers and vast vistas of ever-changing mood and color. Trailhead amenities include an information kiosk and toilet. The lower level of the trail is wheelchair and stroller accessible. The trail can be muddy and slippery if conditions are wet. Signage is informative and well illustrated.

During the summer, actual dinosaur quarrying by paleontologists and volunteers takes place at the Mygatt-Moore quarry, just north of the trail. Folks interested in actively participating in half-day or one-day digs can contact the Museum of Western Colorado.

GETTING THERE: Take I-70 west out of Grand Junction, drive west until you reach exit 2 (2 miles before the Utah-Colorado border). Go north at the exit and in a short distance park at the Trail Through Time parking lot and trailhead.

The trail goes thisaway.

THE ROUTE: After passing through the gate, you will see several informational signs. One offers an overview of the Dinosaur Diamond—a 650 mile tour of sites in Western Colorado and Eastern Utah. Head north on the trail/road where toilets are located to the west. A kiosk with stone pillars provides more detailed information about the quarry and the Jurassic Period geology and dinosaurs.

The Trail Through Time is associated with the Mygatt-Moore Quarry that is just north of the kiosk by about 100 yards. The trail turns east for about 0.2 mile and then divides: veer left for the upper trail, or right for the lower, wheelchair-accessible trail.

The lower trail is an out-and-back hike of about 0.8 mile round trip from the trailhead. The upper trail, to the left, will make a loop connecting with the lower trail after about 1.1 miles.

After a short climb on the upper trail, the first dinosaur skeleton—a Camarasaurus—is visible in the rock matrix. Bronze buttons help identify the bones locked in the sandstone rock.

The trail continues to climb up slightly, through eroded rock, and then passes through a gated fence. After about 0.5 mile, you reach the first of several shelters providing seating, shade, and a

An ancient trail to new discoveries.   PHOTO BY LARRY ALLISON

great view of Rabbit Valley. As the trail descends to a gully, several signs describe desert environments and the geological processes of desert varnish and differential erosion. A well-exposed specimen of Diplodocus vertebrae is soon encountered. An area where a Camptosaurus was excavated appears further down the wash. A section-corner survey marker is within a few feet of this site.

Although the sign indicates that this is the last stop, follow the trail marker to the west to continue the loop back to the junction of the upper and lower trails. Some local mining history is highlighted as the trail approaches another shelter. When the trail connects with the wheelchair-accessible segment, there is a view looking out over Rabbit Valley, with the La Sal Mountains of Utah on the distant horizon. Look for replicas of Cretaceous-era plants along this part of the trail. You will next pass by and around examples of wind and water erosion in a desert environment, demonstrated by a balanced rock and weathered sandstone. The last fossil specimen is a pelvis fragment of a juvenile Sauropod.

The upper and lower trails merge soon, returning you to the kiosk, quarry area, and parking lot.

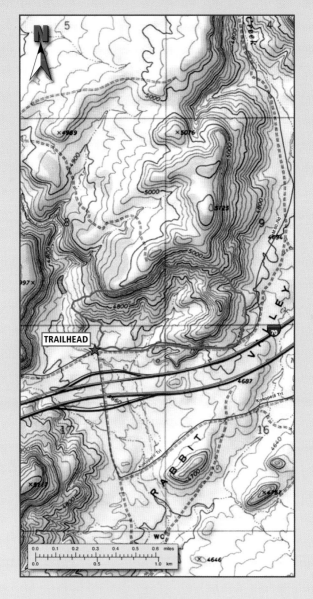

19. Ute Canyon Trail

BY DAVID BUTLER

MAPS	Trails Illustrated, Grand Junction/Fruita, Number 502
ELEVATION LOSS	1,680 feet
RATING	Moderate–difficult
ROUND-TRIP DISTANCE	10.4 miles (recommended as a one-way hike with a car shuttle for a 5.2-mile one-way distance)
ROUND-TRIP TIME	4–5 hours
NEAREST LANDMARK	Rim Rock Drive in the Colorado National Monument

COMMENT: A hike down Ute Canyon, one of the major canyons in the Colorado National Monument, is an ideal outing for those who like quiet and solitude. The hike is one-way from the upper Ute Canyon trail to the Wildwood trailhead. Ute Canyon features towering 200- to 400-foot reddish cliffs of Wingate sandstone and interesting rock formations. You will see a large block of detached Wingate sandstone and an arch during the hike. Most of the canyon bottom is typical high desert vegetation, dominated by juniper and sage.

Except for short, wet sections and stagnant pools, there is little water in the canyon. In spring and early summer, wildflowers and cactus may be in bloom. Listen for the distinct call of a canyon wren; watch for golden eagles and vultures soaring over the cliffs. As you hike down canyon, turn around occasionally and look up canyon to get different perspectives of the natural features.

The trail is fairly well defined and easy to follow. Spring and summer are ideal seasons for this hike. If you hike in summer, get an early start to avoid midday heat. Pets are not allowed on Monument trails.

GETTING THERE: A car shuttle is required, and one vehicle must be left at the Wildwood trailhead. From the 1st and Grand intersection in Grand Junction, proceed west on Grand Avenue, which becomes Hwy 340. Drive over the railroad tracks and the

Looking up Ute Canyon.

PHOTO BY DAVID BUTLER

Colorado River to a left turn at Monument Road. Drive 2.9 miles on Monument Road to South Camp Road and turn right. Go 2.6 miles on South Camp to a T junction and turn left onto South Broadway. After 0.5 mile, turn left onto Wildwood Drive and go another 0.4 mile to the trailhead and parking lot.

To drive to the upper trailhead from Wildwood trailhead, backtrack to the South Camp and Monument Road intersection and turn right onto Monument Road. In 0.6 mile you reach the east entrance station to the Colorado National Monument. Continue another 8.7 miles on Rim Rock Drive to a small parking area at the upper Ute Canyon trailhead. Stay on Rim Rock Drive when you reach the intersection with the Glade Park road. There are no restrooms at either trailhead.

THE ROUTE: From the trailhead, the trail plunges about 550 feet to the canyon bottom in the first 0.5 mile. There is a well-constructed pathway with many steps to facilitate your descent. Fallen Rock, a large block of Wingate sandstone that separated from the cliff, is seen on the left (north) side of the canyon. Past

Spires and balanced rocks are numerous.

PHOTO BY DAVID BUTLER

Fallen Rock, the trail climbs about 100 feet to bypass a gorge eroded into the Precambrian basement rock. Below a towering 400-foot Wingate buttress, the trail bends 90 degrees and heads northeast to descend back down to the canyon bottom.

Over the next 3 miles the trail descends only 300 feet as it meanders down the canyon. In some places, the trail ascends low benches above the stream channel. About a mile below the big bend, the trail passes a large alcove on the north side of the canyon. Just past this alcove, turn around and look back up canyon to see a small arch on the south side of the canyon. Liberty Cap will come into view soon and in another 0.5 mile Grand Mesa will be seen.

As the trail nears Liberty Cap, it bends left, or north, along red slopes and meets the Corkscrew Trail (See Hike No. 7). An option is to hike the Corkscrew Trail to Wildwood. This will add about 0.7 mile to your hike. In another 0.25 mile from this junction, the Ute Canyon Trail meets the Liberty Cap Trail for the last mile back to the Wildwood trailhead.

TRAILHEAD

20. Ute Trail

BY BABS SCHMERLER

MAPS	Trails Illustrated, Black Canyon of the Gunnison NP, Number 245 Curecanti NRA, Black Ridge Quadrangle
ELEVATION GAIN	1,200 feet—after 1,200-foot descent
RATING	Moderate
ROUND-TRIP DISTANCE	9 miles
ROUND-TRIP TIME	4.5–5.5 hours
NEAREST LANDMARK	Olathe turnoff

COMMENT: The Gunnison Gorge Recreation National Conservation Area (NCA) is 62,844 acres of public land administered by the Bureau of Land Management (BLM). The NCA has a diverse landscape, ranging from adobe badlands to rugged piñon- and juniper-covered slopes. At the heart of the NCA, the Gunnison Gorge Wilderness Area encompasses a spectacular black granite and red sandstone double canyon formed by the Gunnison River. The NCA and wilderness area are adjacent to, or are part of, the Black Canyon of the Gunnison National Park. The park itself is worthy of a couple of days of hiking and exploring.

Visitors must register at the trailhead and pay a user fee. For one day, the fee is $3 per person. For one of the four hiker camps at the end of the trail, the fee is $10 per person for one night and $15 per person for two nights. There are no reservations, so it is first come, first served. If you like to fish, bring your gear along.

This trail would offer a good introduction to backpacking for the novice or for younger children, as it is a reasonable length, has designated campsites, and is in easy reach from Montrose or Delta. Ute Trail will take you to the bottom of the Black Canyon. It is the longest trail in the NCA and provides scenic views of the Gunnison River.

GETTING THERE: From Delta, head south on US 50. Look for Carnation Road, about 2.0 miles before the traffic light at the Olathe turnoff. Turn left on Carnation Road to begin the 10.2

Looking down the Gunnison River into the
heart of Black Canyon National Park.

PHOTO BY BABS SCHMERLER

mile drive to the trailhead. In about 2.6 miles, you will come to
6200 Road. Turn left and drive 7.6 miles to the sign designating
the Ute Trail. The final 2.5 miles of this drive is best done with a
high-clearance vehicle, although a Subaru wagon with a capable,
careful driver could probably navigate the road.

From Montrose, go north on US 50 and turn right on Falcon
Road, about 1.0 mile before the Olathe traffic light. There is a
brown Gunnison Gorge NCA sign just after you turn off. The
pavement eventually turns to gravel and you will pass signs for
several other trails—e.g., Chukar, Bobcat, and Duncan. Just
before you get to the turnoff for the Ute Trail, on the right, there is
a sign indicating that you are in Peach Valley. After you turn off
the highway, it is 11.3 miles to the turnoff for the Ute trailhead, a
total of 14 miles from the NCA sign to the trailhead. Again, the
last 2.5 miles are best driven with a high-clearance vehicle.

THE ROUTE: There are covered picnic tables and an outhouse at the
trailhead, and several trails begin here. To access the Ute Trail,
walk between the fee box and kiosk and look about 40 yards
downhill. A brown trail marker will be visible. As you descend,

Large boulders help mark the trail.

PHOTO BY BABS SCHMERLER

an old roadbed is visible to the left and above the trail. The trail gradually winds down below the canyon rim. After 20 to 25 minutes of walking, you will see a horse trough on your left. The trail continues down through several open areas, with desert wildflowers viewable in the spring.

About an hour into the hike, an overlook provides the first views of the Gunnison River. This is a great place to take a break. The trail then winds steeply downward before again gradually descending toward the river. The trail ends at a nice beach with trees. There is a nice camping spot here, or you can go farther downstream to the other marked campsites. Take time to enjoy the bottom of the canyon, and the Gunnison River, as you will now have to retrace your steps and ascend 1,200 feet to your vehicle.

On the way back, near the end of a rock bench, some small hoodoos (chimney-like rock formations) are visible at the end of the bench. At this location there is a spur trail—on the left going down and on the right going up. This appears to go out to some flats and is not part of the official route.

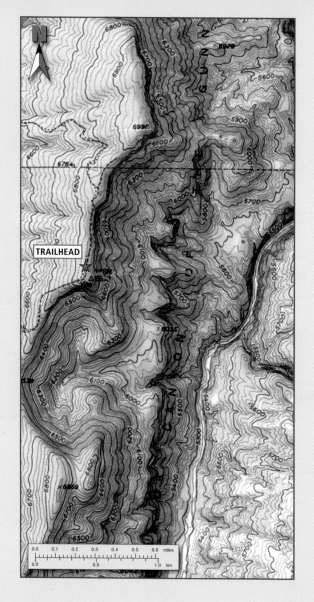

TRAILHEAD

Window Tower Rock with South America Arch,
as found on the Rattlesnake Canyon hike.   PHOTO BY ROD MARTINEZ

PHOTOGRAPHY TIPS

When we are in the outdoors, we see many beautiful subjects that we'd like to remember. Here are a few tips to help you take great photos and enjoy, over and over, the places where you've been:

1. Don't forget to take your camera with you. As you hike, keep it stored within easy reach.

2. Carry plenty of memory cards so you can take enough photographs to properly record your hike and what you saw.

3. Charge your batteries before leaving and take extra ones if you will be out more than one day.

4. Before leaving home, set your camera's resolution to the highest setting possible. Check your manual to see how this is done. Another name for resolution is image quality. You want to use every pixel you paid for when you bought your camera. A higher setting will give you the ability to capture the light and dark tones as well as all the colors your eyes can see.

5. Be prepared. Most hikes start in the early morning, so have your camera out and be prepared to capture the morning light on the mountains or the animals moving around or out of your way.

6. Hold your camera steady. The closer it is to your face, the steadier your camera will be. Your photo should not have that unsteady, out-of-focus look.

7. Place your whole subject in the frame and fill the frame with your subject. If you are taking photos of the mountains, be sure to include the tops. Zoom in to crop out those items that do not add to the photo.

8. I recommend trying vertical photos as opposed to horizontal ones if you are taking photos of trees, flowers, people, or other vertical objects. Vertical will give you the opportunity to increase the size of your subject as you zoom in.

Colorful fall foliage awaits you on the Colorado Mesa.

PHOTO BY ROD MARTINEZ

9. The best way to learn is from your mistakes. Practice, and take lots of photos trying different angles, vertical versus horizontal, as well as different camera settings. Remember, once you buy a memory card, it can be reused—and those pixels are free.

10. If all else fails, read your manual.

WILDLIFE VIEWING TIPS

► **Fade into the woodwork (or woods).** Wear natural colors and unscented lotions, if any. Be as quiet as possible—walk softly, move slowly.

► **Keep to the sidelines.** Watch animals from a distance THEY consider safe. Use binoculars or a telephoto lens to get a closer view. Stay away from nests.

► **Use your senses.**
Eyes. Look up, down, and all around for animal or bird signs such as scat, nests, or tracks. Learn to distinguish these wildlife signatures.
Ears. Listen for animal sounds or movement.
Nose. Be alert to musky scents or strange odors.

► **Think like an animal.** When will an animal eat, nap, drink, or bathe?

► **Optimize your watching.** The ultimate wildlife-watching experience is of animal behaviors—viewing animals without interrupting their normal activities. As a rule, dusk and dawn are the best times for this rewarding viewing.

Pinnacles and rock formations are plentiful
on the Fisher Towers hike. PHOTO BY ROD MARTINEZ

ABOUT THE AUTHOR

 Rod Martinez has always loved being outdoors. As a kid growing up in Cripple Creek, he explored the hills and old mines. As he grew older, Rod found another love—photography. Not quite 18, he left home and, over a period of three weeks, explored and photographed most of our national parks. Rod found it difficult to fully enjoy the national parks in the short movies he had filmed. In time he discovered 35mm photography and a lifelong passion was born.

Rod has climbed 17 of Colorado's 14ers and has hiked in almost all of the Western states, most extensively in Colorado, Utah, and Northern Arizona. As he has hiked, Rod has photographed many beautiful places. His work has resulted in Rod being named Grand Junction's Photographer of the Year for four years in a row.

Rod retired from Sears and now teaches photography and leads photo workshops. He joined Colorado Mountain Club in 2000, has served as the program director, and currently acts as treasurer and trail steward. Rod helped form the Southwest Photographic Arts Association Camera Club 12 years ago. Rod is able to combine his two passions to visually capture nature's beauty on every hike.

CHECKLIST